Friends of the National Library

FORTY YEARS OF THE NATIONAL LIBRARY OF IRELAND SOCIETY

DÓNALL Ó LUANAIGH

ASSOCIATED EDITIONS

on behalf of

THE NATIONAL LIBRARY OF IRELAND SOCIETY

Published by Associated Editions
33 Melrose Avenue, Dublin 3
ISBN 978-1-906429-13-3
www.associatededitions.ie

© Text: Dónall Ó Luanaigh 2010
Dónall Ó Luanaigh has asserted his right under
the Copyright and Related Acts, 2000, to be
identified as the author of this book.
© Photographs: National Library of Ireland
and Private Collections
© Other Images: National Library of Ireland
and original artists.

Copy-edited by Bobbi Reeners
Designed by Vermillion Design, Dublin
Typefaces: ITC Kabel and Adobe Caslon
Printed by Glennon Print, Co. Meath

TABLE OF CONTENTS

Foreword   5

Introduction   7

Chapter 1: 1969–1975   13

Chapter 2: 1976–1988   20

Photographs & Sketches: 1969–2009   27

Chapter 3: 1989–2003   35

Chapter 4: 2004–2010   42

Appendices   46

Sources & Acknowledgements   60

Index   61

To the memory of Patrick Henchy
and his co-founders of the
National Library of Ireland Society

FOREWORD

The National Library of Ireland was established in 1877. Since its establishment, it has had an important role in the cultural and literary life of the country. To help enhance that role, the National Library of Ireland Society was founded in 1969.

The Society was the brain-child of Dr Patrick Henchy, Director of the National Library of Ireland from 1967 to 1976. He and those who joined him at the inaugural meeting were clear about the mission of the Society. It was "to harness the tremendous amount of goodwill towards the National Library" and thus promote interest in it and provide support for its various activities. With this same aim, librarians of other Irish libraries have participated in the work of the Society throughout its history. Among these were Desmond Clarke, of the Royal Dublin Society; Muriel McCarthy, of Archbishop Marsh's Library; and Peter Costello, of the Central Catholic Library.

In this meticulously researched monograph, Dónall Ó Luanaigh notes the publications sponsored by the Society. He records the financial support the Society has provided for the Library and, on occasion, for the recreational activities of its staff. He highlights the constructive proposals forwarded to the relevant authorities at different times for improving the Library's facilities and administrative structures.

Nor, as the author states, has the Society been negligent in organising activities for its members. Its lectures, book launches, outings and film screenings are all duly reported. A valuable appendix lists the lectures presented under the auspices of the Society. The author's naming of those who have been associated with the Society reads like a roll-call of the great and the good of Ireland's literary and cultural life across two generations.

To a large extent, the success of the Society has depended on its relationship with the Library's Directors. For the most part, these tended to be satisfactory and workmanlike, though no Director was as enthusiastic a supporter of the Society as Dr Henchy. As a member of the Library staff and long-serving member of the Executive Committee of the Society, the author was admirably placed to deal with this topic, which he does with characteristic sensitivity.

Ó Luanaigh illustrates the manner in which the Society over the years has encouraged and facilitated the acquisition by the Library of valuable material and gives as the most recent example a rare seventeenth-century atlas presented by Annraí Ó Braonáin and his wife.

The author formally acknowledges generous donations to the Society by the Allberry, Brown and O'Meara families. Nor does he fail to commend long-serving members of the Society's Executive Committee and those who have significantly contributed to its activities. Not least among these are Nora Ní Shiúlliobháin, Gerard Lyne and the mercurial Felix Larkin. He notes the present vigorous state of the Society with a membership of 550, its highest ever.

This overview of the first forty years of the National Library of Ireland Society is pleasingly benign and comprehensive. The author's references to some well-known characters will bring a smile of recognition to the faces of many readers. All friends of the National Library will find the narrative fascinating. Dónall Ó Luanaigh is to be thanked and congratulated for what was obviously, for him, a labour of love.

J. Anthony Gaughan
Chairman, National Library of Ireland Society
September 2010

INTRODUCTION

The National Library Society is a model of its kind. Formed by disinterested enthusiasts who are properly informed and satisfied to help to promote the Library and its objects without seeking to obtrude themselves upon the actual working of the institution by the staff, they give an example which could well be emulated in other fields.

Irish Times, 25 October 1976

On the evening of 16 October 1969, a meeting took place in the lecture theatre of the National Gallery of Ireland, Dublin, at which the National Library of Ireland Society was founded. It was from the outset, and has remained, an association of "friends" of the National Library. This short history celebrates its first forty years.

The Society had its origins in an idea of Patrick Henchy, who had become Director of the National Library of Ireland two years previously in 1967. From his experience as Keeper of Printed Books, Henchy had become aware of the very grave needs of the Library because of poor funding by successive governments since 1922. His visits, as Director, to other national libraries in the United Kingdom and elsewhere in Europe, and his contacts with the heads of these repositories, had confirmed to him that the National Library of Ireland had much ground to make up in matters of adequate staffing and storage, purchasing funds and conservation facilities. Henchy saw the need for a support group, independent of the public service, which would be made up of academics and authors, as well as ordinary users of the Library, from both Ireland and overseas.

The Society is twenty years older than the Friends of the British Library, while the Friends of the National Collections of Ireland was founded by Sarah Purser in 1924 and the Friends of the Library of Trinity College Dublin dates from 1946. These bodies all have among their objectives the acquisition of artworks, books, manuscripts and similar items for the appropriate repositories. This has not been the practice so far of the National Library of Ireland Society. From hearsay evidence, it would appear that Richard James Hayes (Patrick Henchy's predecessor as Director of the National Library, from 1940 to 1967) attempted to organise a voluntary support group for the Library in the USA during the 1940s. This effort, unfortunately, came to nothing. The objectives of the Society as set out in its constitution, to "assist and support the National Library of Ireland in the maintenance and protection of its services...", do not preclude the purchasing of rare books, manuscripts and other suitable items for presentation to the Library. To date, however, the National Library of Ireland Society has been mainly concerned with effectively mobilising the large amount of goodwill that exists towards the Library and with fostering that goodwill by arranging public lectures and film shows dealing with various aspects of the Library's collections.

The first Executive Committee of the new Society was chaired by Patrick Lynch, the eminent economist, and included scholars such as David Greene (who had begun his career on the professional staff of the Library), as well as American academics who specialised in Irish studies such as Richard Ellmann and Eoin McKiernan. Senator Michael Yeats was also a founding member. The Chief Justice, Cearbhall Ó Dálaigh, agreed to act as patron of the Society. Ó Dálaigh remained as patron until he became President of Ireland in 1974. He was succeeded by Patrick Henchy. The Society has had no patron since Henchy died in 2001. A constitution for the Society, devised by Ciarán Mac An Ailí, a lawyer and bibliophile, was adopted.

Patrick Henchy became the first Honorary Secretary of the Society. On resigning from the post of Director in 1976 to become Director of the Chester Beatty Library and Gallery of Oriental Art, he also resigned from the post of Secretary of the Society. He was succeeded by Alf Mac Lochlainn, also his successor as Director of the Library. A little later, it was decided that it was inappropriate to nominate people to the Executive Committee who were not resident in Ireland or, if living here, were unable to attend meetings regularly. This policy has been followed ever since. Nevertheless, membership of the Society continues to include people who live outside Ireland.

Within a few years of its foundation, the Society had up to 500 members. Figures have fluctuated, but there are currently about 550 members. More than twenty years ago, it was decided that honorary membership of the Society should be conferred on retired members of the Library's staff. This move has helped to preserve contact with former colleagues, many of whom have participated in the Society's lectures and tours.

From the beginning, librarians of other Irish libraries have participated generously in the work of the Society. The second Chairman of the Society was Desmond Clarke, Librarian of the Royal Dublin Society (which was itself the parent body of the National Library). Muriel McCarthy, Librarian of Archbishop Marsh's Library, was Vice-Chairman for many years. Also, Peter Costello, Honorary Librarian of the Central Catholic Library, has been a loyal supporter of Society events for decades. Maurice J. Craig, the eminent architectural historian and authority on the history of Irish bookbindings, combined his membership of the Library's Council of Trustees with active membership of the Executive Committee over many years, acting as Vice-Chairman of the Executive Committee for a considerable period.

In addition to those already mentioned, the Society has been fortunate in having had a succession of distinguished Chairmen over the years: Eric T.D. Lambert, administrator, diplomat and historian; Henry A. Wheeler, archaeologist; J.W. de Courcy, civil engineering professor and historian; Margaret Mac Curtain, historian, Dominican nun and feminist; and its current Chairman, Fr J. Anthony Gaughan PP, historian and biographer.

Throughout its history, the Society has worked in collaboration with successive Directors of the Library to highlight the Library's needs. Sometimes, this collaboration has been closer than on other occasions. Happily, many of the concerns often expressed by the Society have been redressed in the recent years of economic prosperity, particularly with regard to adequate staffing and conservation facilities. However, provision of adequate storage space remains a critical problem. In the early years, lectures were delivered under the Society's auspices by the heads of the British Library and the other two national libraries in the United Kingdom. These lectures were meant to demonstrate the amount of catching up which the National Library of Ireland had to do in order to be on a par with these repositories. Moreover, in order to outline the needs of the Library, a delegation from the Executive Committee was received by John Bruton TD, later Taoiseach, and more recently EU Ambassador to the USA, who was then Parliamentary Secretary to the Minister for Education with responsibility for the National Library.

Almost from its foundation, the Society instituted an annual programme of public lectures on subjects broadly related to the Library and its collections, including literary readings and film shows. These lectures have dealt with a very wide variety of subjects. In the early twentieth century, there were many such lecture-organising societies in Ireland. However, the advent of sound and visual broadcasting has resulted in their virtual disappearance – except where there is a specific subject focus. Lecturers such as Roy Foster, Maurice Harmon, Declan Kiberd and Fr Liam Swords have all remarked favourably on the quality and the "interestedness" of the audience at the lectures held by the National Library Society, Kiberd noting that a typical audience might include PhD students as well as people just passing by. Because the Library itself had no lecture theatre until 2004, these events were mostly held outside the Library in a variety of locations in central Dublin. In addition to the National Gallery of Ireland, these have included the Royal Irish Academy, the Royal College of Surgeons in Ireland, the Physics Theatre at UCD in Earlsfort Terrace, and the now-defunct Carroll's Theatre at Grand Parade.

Over the years, lecturers have included poets such as Eavan Boland, Nobel laureate Seamus Heaney, Brendan Kennelly and Michael Longley; novelists John Banville, Jennifer Johnston and Benedict Kiely; historians Brendan Bradshaw, Roy Foster, Tom Garvin, Michael Laffan and Joe Lee; and Gaelic scholars Gearóid Denvir and Nessa Ní Shéaghdha – as well as most senior members of the staff of the Library and the Genealogical Office/Office of Arms. Irish film directors Kieran Hickey, Neil Jordan, Muiris Mac Conghail and Seán Ó Mórdha have all shown their films to the Society, providing personal introductions and commentaries.

A list of these lectures and film shows forms an appendix to this work. Also included in separate appendices are lists of the Richard Irvine Best Memorial Lectures and the John J. O'Meara Memorial Lectures. While the former (which, incidentally, also began in 1969) are the responsibility of the Board of the Library, the Society has, in the words of its Honorary Secretary in 1998, "acted as facilitator in the matter of publicity and organisation [and these lectures] feature on the Society's programme". The O'Meara Lectures, which began in 2005, are given more directly under the auspices of the Society and have been made possible by a generous endowment from the family of the late John O'Meara, Professor of Latin at UCD from 1948 to 1984.

From the mid-1980s, the Society has organised an annual summer tour to libraries, historic buildings and other sites throughout the island of Ireland. The first of these visits was to the King's Inns, Dublin, in 1986.

A recent (2009) tour to the Boyne valley gives a flavour of these events. The Society visited Beaulieu House, the Francis Ledwidge Museum in Slane and Larchill Arcadian Garden, a *ferme ornée* dating from the seventeenth century. At the Ledwidge Museum, Gerard Lyne, recently retired as Keeper of Manuscripts in the Library and a former Honorary Secretary of the Society, read some of Ledwidge's poems – a moving and memorable experience for all present. These tours have been very popular and early booking has been essential in order to be sure of a place. Jack Hyland, a keen supporter of Society events for many years, has left us his own photographic record of several tours.

The late Michael Hewson was the third and last Director of the National Library to act as Honorary Secretary. Since 1983, the post has been filled by other senior members of the Library's staff, a notable one being Gerard Lyne. Lyne was Assistant Secretary from 1984 until he was appointed Honorary Secretary in 1991, remaining on until 1998. As a historian, he was able to call on many eminent colleagues to give papers to the Society and to speak to papers. Further, because of his interest in, and appreciation of, contemporary Irish literature, the Society was privileged to hear from many of the leading writers of the day. The rapport with poets and novelists achieved in these years has borne fruit in the Library's remarkable success in acquiring many major literary archives during Lyne's term as Keeper of Manuscripts.

The position of Honorary Treasurer of the Society has always been filled by a member who is not on the Library staff. The Society has been very well served in this role by the late Nóra Ní Shúilliobháin and the late Dermot Blunden, and, more recently by Ciarán Ó hÓgartaigh, Felix M. Larkin and Ian d'Alton (the current Treasurer). From the outset, the Society was mainly dependent for its finances on members' subscriptions. In 1986 and 1987, however, the Society, through the good offices of Dr Henchy, was the recipient of a splendid bequest from Mrs Wanda Petronella Brown, wife of book collector and lawyer, J. Barry Brown, of Naas, Co. Kildare. This gift has enabled the Society to adopt a progressive attitude towards publications and other worthy endeavours requiring the expenditure of significant money. Over many years the Society has also given some financial assistance to the Library and its staff in the organisation of social events.

Even in today's difficult circumstances it is hard to credit that the Library was once very restricted financially regarding what it might be able to publish. The Society led the way here with a number of interesting monographs on the history and collections of the Library and the Office of

Arms based on lectures delivered to the Society. Authors included Patrick Henchy himself and his successor, Alf Mac Lochlainn. In addition, during the period that has recently come to be called the "first recession" – the 1980s – the Society came to the Library's rescue financially on more than one occasion. The sums involved, while small, covered projects which were vitally urgent and for which funding would not otherwise have been immediately available.

On a sombre note, it may well be that the Irish and worldwide recession which began in late 2007, with the consequent draconian reductions in public spending, will result in the National Library of Ireland Society becoming more relevant than ever before in its history as the champion of the Library's needs. In any event, the Society remains active in promoting the Library's interests and continues to attract lively, imaginative and intelligent people to its Executive Committee. Chief among these in recent years is Felix Larkin, currently Vice-Chairman, who has edited the Society's most recent publication *Librarians, Poets and Scholars* (Four Courts Press, 2007) which includes many essays which had their origin in lectures delivered to the Society.

For me, impressions of the Society could be summed up by Dryden's phrase, "to delight and instruct". *Thar gach aon rud, is léir dom an meas a bhí (agus atá) ag an oiread sin daoine ar an Leabharlann Náisiúnta. Cuimhním ar Pheadar O'Donnell, úrscéalaí agus réabhlóidí, ag teacht ar chúirt chugainn chun labhairt linn, cé go raibh sé aosta ag an am. Cuimhním freisin ar Lorna Reynolds a bhí ar tí léacht a thabhairt dúinn nuair a thárla taisme di. Is ar éigean a raibh biseach uirthi gur tháinig sí agus thug sár-léacht dúinn. Nuair a tháinig Seamus Heaney in ár measc, bhí slua óganach ghá síor-cheistiú ag deire an thráthnóna. Dar leis an file, áfach, b'é sin an chuid den ócáid as a bhain sé an-taithneamh is mó!* [1]

Dónall Ó Luanaigh

---

[1]   Above all else, I appreciate the regard people had (and have) for the National Library. I recall Peadar O'Donnell, novelist and revolutionary, coming to address us, even though he was then advanced in years. I also recall Lorna Reynolds, who was about to lecture to us when she suffered an accident. Hardly had she recovered, when she arrived and gave an excellent lecture. When Seamus Heaney came among us, a crowd of young people posed him questions unceasingly towards the end of the evening. According to the poet, however, this was the part of the event that he enjoyed most!

CHAPTER I: 1969–1975

Patrick Henchy, Director of the National Library of Ireland, sent out a circular letter dated 6 October 1969 giving notice of a meeting to be held at the National Gallery of Ireland, Merrion Square, Dublin, on Thursday, 16 October. The purpose of the meeting, organised by "a number of friends of the National Library", was to establish a National Library of Ireland Society. The letter went on to say that the main object of this Society would be "to promote interest in the Library and help it achieve its aims as a national institution".

The meeting duly took place on the date announced, with an attendance of 250 or so. Present were Bruce Arnold, Máire Comerford, Tomás de Bhaldraithe, Alan Eager (later Librarian of the Royal Dublin Society), Fr Francis Finegan SJ, G.A. Hayes-McCoy, Máire Cruise O'Brien and Hilary Pyle. In addition to Senator Michael Yeats, the following members of the Oireachtas were present: Gerard L'Estrange TD, Senator Eoin Ryan and Senator Owen Sheehy Skeffington.

The meeting, which attracted significant press coverage, was addressed by Patrick Lynch, Professor of Political Economy at UCD. Lynch had made an important contribution to the formulation of official policy on economic development and education in Ireland, and was Chairman of Aer Lingus and a member of the Higher Education Authority. In the course of his address, he stated that there was a "tremendous amount of goodwill towards the National Library as a national institution" and that the object of the Society would be to harness this goodwill. He drew attention to the number of valuable books and original manuscripts which were leaving Ireland. The Society, he said, would also act a means of communication between the public and Library management.

Senator Michael Yeats formally proposed the foundation of the National Library of Ireland Society. The proposal was seconded by Desmond Clarke, Librarian of the Royal Dublin Society. Robert O'Driscoll, of the University of Toronto, also spoke in support of the motion, which was carried unanimously.

Following this, it was decided to set up "a small working committee to prepare rules etc. for the Society". This committee consisted of the following:

Chair: Patrick Lynch

Secretary: Patrick Henchy (Director of the National Library)

Committee: Senator Michael B. Yeats, Desmond Clarke, Captain Tadhg McGlinchey, H.W. Parke (of TCD), Margot Chubb (of the Library, TCD), Ellen Power (Librarian of UCD), Máirín O'Byrne (Dublin City and County Librarian), C.S. Andrews, Maurice Harmon (of UCD) and David Greene (of the School of Celtic Studies at the Dublin Institute of Advanced Studies)

The degree of cooperation with other Dublin libraries may be seen from this list. Also, the inclusion of C.S. Andrews formed a link between the Society and those who had been active during the earlier years of the State.

Maurice Harmon, then of UCD, is the last surviving founder-member of the Executive Committee. He resigned after some years owing to pressure of work, but returned to the Committee in the 1990s. He has lectured to the Society on a number of occasions, and has also responded to several papers. In the course of a letter to the Honorary Secretary a few years ago, he noted: "They are a good audience, you can feel the attention…".

The Committee met within a couple of weeks of the inaugural meeting and decided to form a National Committee consisting of prominent people from at home and abroad, including the following: Colm Ó hEocha (of UCG), Ciarán Mac An Ailí (solicitor, civil liberties activist and rare book collector), Kenneth Darwin (Director of the Public Record Office of Northern Ireland), and Richard Ellmann (biographer of Joyce and Yeats). Ciarán Mac An Ailí was asked to prepare a constitution for the Society, which was approved. Mac An Ailí's collection of travel literature is now one of the treasures of the library at the University of Limerick.

It was also decided to request the Chief Justice, Cearbhall Ó Dálaigh, to act as patron of the Society. This request was acceded to, and the Chief Justice remained patron until he became President of Ireland. In April 1984 Patrick Henchy agreed to become the Society's patron.

Among other members of the early Executive Committees were: Tom Barrington (founder of the Institute of Public Administration), Eoin McKiernan (President of the Irish-American Cultural Institute), John

J. O'Meara (today the Society administers the lecture series set up in his memory) and Irene Calvert. Calvert had a career as a senior public servant both in Northern Ireland and the Republic, and was an Independent MP at Stormont from 1945 to 1953, representing the Queen's University constituency.

The early Executive Committees also included Robert Cussen, the noted book collector from Co. Limerick, and Gerald Goldberg, sometime Lord Mayor of Cork. In the course of a letter to Henchy, Cussen stressed the importance of the Society "as the average man has no concept of what the National Library has to offer".

Though not a member of the Executive Committee, Edward MacLysaght, Chairman of the Irish Manuscripts Commission, and formerly Chief Herald and Keeper of Manuscripts at the Library, played an active part in the Society during its early years. MacLysaght had been a member of the Irish Convention in 1917 and also a member of the Free State Senate in the 1920s. Among the early members of the Society was Eileen McCarville (formerly of UCD) who had been a member of Cumann na mBan during the War of Independence.

Veronica McEvatt recalls that Garret FitzGerald TD (afterwards Taoiseach) was supportive of the Society in its early days, while Margaret Mac Curtain remembers similar background support coming from the historian, T. Desmond Williams.

Henchy had assembled what Michael Hewson, a later Director, was to describe as a "prestigious group of patrons" to get the Society off to a flying start. By early 1970, 15,000 publicity brochures for the Society had been printed, with 10,000 of these distributed in the USA through the kindness of Eoin McKiernan, President of the Irish-American Cultural Institute. McKiernan also made a plea for the Library in the Institute's periodical *Éire-Ireland*. During the first year of its existence, the Society recruited 475 members.

Membership subscription of the Society was originally fixed at £1 per annum. The present subscription rates are as follows: ordinary membership – €25 (Senior citizens, €15; Students, €10); and corporate membership (by invitation only) – €1,000. A generous financial donation to help with the founding of the Society was given by Sir John Galvin, who avoided all publicity at the time for this kindness.

Kenneth W. Humphreys (successively librarian of the University of Birmingham and of the European University Institute in Florence), who had been engaged as a consultant to advise on the development of the Library, was approached with regard to addressing the Society at an early date. This address was given on 19 November 1970, following the Society's first Annual General Meeting. In 1972 Humphreys lectured on the Library on Radio Éireann as part of the Thomas Davis Lecture series. During its first few years, Patrick Henchy also gave a lecture to the Society on the history of the National Library and its collections, while Maurice J. Craig, a member of the Library's Council of Trustees, lectured on historic Irish bookbindings.

Much of the time during the Executive Committee meetings of these early years was concerned with the failure of the Department of Education to publish Dr Humphreys' report on the Library. Unfortunately, this report – which recommended major improvements for the Library – was never published by the government. The wider issue of governmental neglect of the Library was aired at AGMs of the National Library Society. For example, writing in the *Irish Independent* of 11 December 1972, Bruce Arnold described the conflict at an AGM, albeit courteously carried on, between the "hawks" and the "doves" (i.e. those critical of the ongoing governmental neglect of the Library and those who were more optimistic on this score).

By 1974 the Society had heard lectures from the Director of the British Library and the Librarians of the National Libraries of Scotland and Wales. These lectures demonstrated the huge disparity in facilities, accommodation and staffing that existed between the National Library of Ireland and its counterparts on the neighbouring island. From his correspondence with these lecturers, it is clear that Henchy had formed a good working relationship with heads of other national libraries.

When Professor Lynch resigned as Chairman towards the end of 1972, he was succeeded by Desmond Clarke, Librarian of the Royal Dublin Society. Lynch was made an Honorary Life Member of the Society in recognition of (in Henchy's words) "doing so much to set it [the Society] on its feet". With regard to the appointment of Clarke as Chairman, it should be remembered that the National Library of Ireland owes its existence in large measure to the Royal Dublin Society.

Nóra Ní Shúilliobháin joined the Executive Committee in January 1973, becoming Honorary Treasurer a short time later. She would continue in that role until 1990, an unrivalled record of service to the Society. A one-time official of the Department of Education, Ní Shúilliobháin is perhaps best known from her contribution, with Eoin O'Mahony, to the Radio

Éireann programme *Meet the Clans*. Broadcast during the early 1960s, it led to a widespread popular interest in Irish family history and genealogy.

In late 1973 a delegation from the Society's Executive Committee met with John Bruton TD, Parliamentary Secretary to the Minister for Education with responsibility for *inter alia* the Library. This meeting took place at Bruton's request. A memo prepared by Desmond Clarke in advance of the meeting began as follows:

> While many of the members of the National Library of Ireland Society are writers, scholars and of the learned professions, others are simply people with an interest in our cultural heritage which is so much part of the National Library.

The memo included proposals that the former National College of Art building should be refurbished for the use of the Library, and also that the Library should be made an independent semi-State body. Both proposals have now been implemented, though this has only occurred during the last ten years or so. The Society's recommendations did eventually bear fruit! As far as can be traced, this was the only occasion on which members of the Society officially met with a government minister holding responsibility for the Library.

It was Bruton who initiated the policy of travelling exhibitions and educational publications based on the collections of the national cultural institutions. This work was undertaken for the Library, with great success, by Noel Kissane, Education Officer and later Keeper of Manuscripts.

The Society assisted in the publication and distribution of the text of the Richard Irvine Best Memorial Lecture delivered on 18 May 1973 by Brian Ó Cuív on the subject of *The Irish Bardic Duanaire or "Poem Book"*. This lecture series was funded by an American academic to commemorate Best, fourth librarian of the National Library and Gaelic scholar. Although the Best Lectures are the responsibility of the Library itself, the Society has consistently publicised these events and included them in its programme. It was the Executive Committee which recommended that Michael Holroyd might be asked to deliver the Best lecture on G.B. Shaw on the fiftieth anniversary of the dramatist's death in 2000. The Society also facilitated the 2009 Best lecture given by Robert P. Schmuhl, of Notre Dame University, on *Easter 1916 and America: a provisional appraisal*. A list of the Best lectures to date is given in Appendix 2.

On 11 May 1974 a ceremony took place at the grave of Jasper Robert Joly at Clonbulloge, Co. Offaly, when the Society honoured Joly (the donor of the Library's core collection of books) with an inscription on his gravestone, acknowledging his generosity. An address was given by the Director of the Library, Patrick Henchy. It appears that the idea for this ceremony was put forward by Sybil Le Brocquy, author and member of the Council of Trustees of the Library, who was an early supporter of the Society.

In 1975 the Society sponsored an exhibition in the Library of plans and photographs of national library buildings from various countries. Also in 1975, the Society sponsored the publication of a new edition, by Michael Hewson, of the *Catalogue of Irish Topographical Prints and Drawings [in the] National Library of Ireland*, the first edition of which, edited by Rosalind M. Elmes, had appeared in 1943.

In order to publicise the Library's collections and activities, the Society decided in 1974 to commission Kieran Hickey to make a film on the Library. Hickey had previously been associated with the Library through his two films *Faithful Departed* (concerned with James Joyce, and based on the photographs of Dublin in the Library's Lawrence Collection) and *The Light of Other Days* (a general view of Ireland as depicted in the Lawrence Collection). Both of these films gave great publicity to the Lawrence Collection of photographs which, although acquired by the Library during the years of the Second World War, was largely unused and unexploited until these films were made. Books by Maurice Gorham and others also revealed the richness and diversity of these photographs to the public at large in showing the country as it was before the major social and political changes brought about by the events of 1914 to 1923.

The Society sought and received generous sponsorship for Hickey's film *Portrait of a Library* from the Bank of Ireland, and the film had its premiere at the National Gallery of Ireland in October 1976. Maurice Craig wrote the script for the film and the commentary was spoken by Cyril Cusack, the doyen of the Irish stage. Music for the film was selected by John Beckett and played by him on a Victorian piano and on a harpsichord made by Cathal Gannon. Irish writers Mary Lavin, Edna O'Brien and Sean O'Faolain were interviewed on-screen. Copies of the film were sent to Irish embassies abroad and the film was shown on RTÉ television. The Bank of Ireland saw its role of sponsoring the film as "bringing to greater public notice the … work of the Library … and encouraging people to use [the Library]".

In the course of his address at the film's premiere, Desmond Clarke emphasised the need for "a strong and vocal group of people to work [on behalf of the Library] outside the tightly circumscribed circle of government interference and government tardiness and apparent lack of interest". That, of course, was – and remains – the *raison d'être* of the Society. On the same occasion, Patrick Lynch spoke of the Library as "not just a stately mausoleum but … the custodian of the cultural heritage of a nation".

CHAPTER 2: 1976–1988

A critical development in the Society's fortunes took place in 1976 when Patrick Henchy resigned from his post as Director of the Library to become Director of the Chester Beatty Library and Gallery of Oriental Art. At the same time he resigned from the post of Honorary Secretary of the Society, although he remained on the Executive Committee for some time after this and was to be responsible for the Wanda Petronella Brown bequest to the Society in the 1980s. The Society was Henchy's creation. He had carefully chosen its senior figures and, subtly and tactfully, charted its course. Never again would relations be as close between the Society and the management of the Library.

The Society lost another key figure in 1976 when Captain Tadhg McGlinchey died as the result of a car accident. A well-known publisher, he had been an active member of the Executive Committee from the outset and had had an important role in the production of the Society's first publicity brochure and in the publication of Professor Ó Cuív's R.I. Best Lecture.

Alf Mac Lochlainn succeeded Patrick Henchy both as Director of the Library and as Honorary Secretary of the Society. Unlike Henchy, Mac Lochlainn felt that it was best for Library management to keep this voluntary body, or "supporters' club", at arm's length. Perhaps a football analogy might best illustrate this attitude. The job specification for Jack Charlton, Kevin Heffernan or Declan Kidney must be to make sure the best players are on their respective teams, out on the field and winning the matches. The team managers must not concern themselves unduly with acting as cheerleaders of the fans. That was Mac Lochlainn's attitude, and it was shared in varying degrees by each of the Directors who succeeded him.

However, if Directors tended to adopt a less "hands-on" approach to the Society from 1976 onward, the number of members of senior Library staff serving on the Committee has increased over the years. This extracurricular activity came to be seen as a mark of particular commitment to the Library by younger staff members aspiring to the most senior roles in the Library's structure. Moreover, Noel Kissane, the Library's first Education Officer, and later Keeper of Manuscripts, while never serving on the Executive Committee himself, always recognised the importance of the Society in what is now termed "outreach". He was thus constantly on hand to give sound advice.

In 1978 Mac Lochlainn advised the Executive Committee that it seemed no longer necessary to have persons on the Committee who, while generous with their patronage, were unable to attend meetings, being resident outside Ireland. This policy change was adopted and has been followed ever since, although the Society continues to welcome members resident outside Ireland. The overseas members have been mostly American scholars who have spent some time in Ireland using the Library's resources.

Desmond Clarke, the second Chairman of the Executive Committee, died in 1979. As well as being Librarian of the Royal Dublin Society, he was the author of a number of historical biographies, including lives of Richard Lovell Edgeworth and Thomas Prior. His new edition of Stephen Brown's *Ireland in Fiction* was published posthumously in 1985. He was a member of the Council of Trustees of the National Library.

Eric T.D. Lambert was the next Chairman. After a career in British administration overseas, as an army officer in the Far East during the Second World War and as an adviser in the British diplomatic service in South America (a career which, in his own words, had brought him from "Timbuktu to Kathmandu"), Lambert had retired to his native Dublin to work on the history of the Irish volunteers in Bolivar's movement for independence in Venezuela during the first quarter of the nineteenth century. His research on this topic has been published in Spanish in a number of volumes. While a member of the Executive Committee, he spoke at one of the Society's AGMs praising the work of the Library Assistants and urging that a proper scheme of career development should be implemented for this grade of staff.

Lambert was succeeded as Chairman by J.B. Malone, author of the well-known guide book *Walking in Wicklow*. "J.B.", as he was generally known, was also the author of many newspaper articles dealing with Dublin's historic buildings and landmarks. His collection of photographs, taken during his walks in the Dublin and Wicklow mountains, is now deposited in the Library's Photographic Archive.

Henry A. Wheeler (who had been President of the Royal Society of Antiquaries of Ireland and was also President of the Cambrian Society) took over as Chairman in 1982, remaining in office until 1992. A brilliant student at Cambridge and at Trinity College Dublin, Wheeler had been an archaeologist with the Office of Public Works. He was the co-author with Maurice J. Craig of *Dublin City Churches of the Church of Ireland.*

A perusal of the minutes of the Executive Committee during the early 1980s indicates that there were certain tensions between the Committee and Library management. There is mention of the danger of a conflict of interest between the role of Director of the National Library and that of Honorary Secretary of the Society. There was also a subtle change of emphasis in the affairs of the Society, with its business consisting increasingly of the organisation of lectures to which members of the general public, as well as members, were invited. A drop of 100 from the 1977 total in Society membership was recorded in September 1980. At all times, however, the minutes of the Executive Committee show a concern shared with the Library's Director and Council of Trustees for the well-being and progress of the Library. In particular, the Executive Committee was exercised about such matters as the lack of conservation facilities in the Library, inadequate accommodation and poor staffing levels. During these years and later on, a specific and recurring concern at meetings of the Executive Committee and at AGMs was with the unfilled vacancy in the post of Inspector of Manuscripts in the Library since the death in 1981 of Sir John Ainsworth, Bart.

In November 1981 the Genealogical Office was obliged to vacate its premises at Dublin Castle (which had been its location and that of its predecessor, the Office of the Ulster King of Arms, for the best part of two hundred years) owing to safety concerns with regard to the building. Thus, during 1981 and 1982, the Executive Committee anxiously monitored delays in the refurbishment of the premises at Nos. 2 and 3 Kildare Street, part of the former Kildare Street Club building, which had been acquired for the Library by the Office of Public Works to house the Library's Department of Manuscripts and the Genealogical Office/Office of Arms. As this matter dragged on, the Executive Committee of the Society corresponded in 1987 with John Wilson TD, a former Minister for Education who was then Minister for Tourism and Transport. Wilson was a member of the Society and attended several of its lectures over the years.

Letters from two Chairmen of the Society highlighting these and other urgent Library needs were published in the *Irish Times* – a letter from Desmond Clarke on 3 March 1976 and letters from Henry Wheeler on 16 March 1984, 19 March 1987 and 29 May 1989. Clarke's letter referred to the "unsatisfactory conditions under which the National Library of Ireland functions, conditions that would not be tolerated or accepted in any other country". In 1984 Wheeler decried "the neglect which the Library has suffered down the years in the hands of successive Ministers for Education" and he urged "the government to examine and take appropriate steps to deal with the Library's long-tem future development". His 1987 and 1989 letters were about accommodation issues, and in the second of these he stated that "the Library, which has developed and expanded over the past 100 years, cannot operate adequately in its present restricted accommodation".

In 1981, the death occurred of David Greene (Dáithí Ó hUaithne), a prominent founder-member of the Society. Greene's career had begun as an Assistant Librarian at the National Library. He was Professor of Irish at Trinity College Dublin, subsequently holding a chair in the School of Celtic Studies at the Dublin Institute of Advanced Studies.

Alf Mac Lochlainn resigned from the post of Honorary Secretary of Society in the spring of 1982. Simultaneously he resigned from the directorship of the Library to become librarian of University College Galway. Mac Lochlainn was succeeded in both posts by Michael Hewson. One year later, Hewson resigned as Secretary to be succeeded by Dónall Ó Luanaigh, Keeper of Printed Books. Ó Luanaigh remained as Secretary until 1991, being greatly assisted throughout his period in office by Gerard Lyne (historian and co-editor of *The Correspondence of Daniel O'Connell*), who was then Assistant Keeper of Manuscripts. Lyne, who retired in May 2009 as the Library's Keeper of Manuscripts, was Honorary Secretary of the Society from 1991 to 1998.

From 1983 onwards the practice began of arranging lectures and literary readings to the Society by contemporary poets and novelists, though historical and bibliographical subjects and some recently made Irish documentary films still featured in the annual programme. Speakers during the 1980s included Seamus Heaney, Brendan Kennelly and Benedict Kiely. A full list of lectures and other events to date is given in Appendix 1.

Active members of the Executive Committee during the early 1980s included Ciarán Blair, Brian Fitzelle, Kathleen Garvin, John M. Gilmartin,

Veronica McEvatt, Statia McGartoll, Edward More O'Ferrall KM, Gréagóir Ó Dúill, David Rose and Julian Walton. Mrs McEvatt had acted as Honorary Treasurer for a short time in the early days of the Society and remained on as a member of the Committee for many years. Mr Blair, a civil engineer and sometime President of Cumann na n-Innealtóirí, made many proposals for the regeneration of both the Library itself and the Society. However, after some time he appeared to have become disillusioned with the conservatism he perceived in some of his colleagues on the Committee, if not also in the Library management, and resigned from the Committee in 1984. Dr Gilmartin, an art historian, later became Chairperson of the Friends of the National Collections. Gréagóir Ó Dúill is a poet and historian. David Rose organised an Oscar Wilde summer school in Ireland for some years. Although Rose, Brian Fitzelle and Julian Walton all resigned from the Committee when they ceased to reside in Dublin, they remained actively interested in the welfare of the Society and of the Library for quite some time afterwards.

Although not members of the Committee, the following were also strong supporters of the Society during these years: Stephen Kearney, who had been Secretary General of the Department of Defence; Monica Nevin, who contributed papers to the *Journal of the Royal Society of Antiquaries of Ireland*; and Cornelius F. Smith, author of several books on Irish social and transport history.

No account of the Society would be complete without a reference to E. Maitland Woolf. Fr Gaughan, in his book *Recollections of a Writer by Accident*, recalls his impressions of the National Library and the Society and includes a very accurate description of Woolf as "an eccentric bookseller and a genuine and practical friend of the [National] Library". Woolf had apparently studied law during his youth and believed himself to be an expert on legal matters. At any rate, he would arrive at every AGM from the foundation of the Society until his death during the 1980s armed with queries as to whether or not the proceedings of the meeting were being held in accordance with the Society's constitution. Also, he went through the Treasurer's report in detail. However, as soon as the AGM was over, his aggressive "Mr Hyde" demeanour completely disappeared and – at least until the next AGM came around – he would come along to the Society's lectures, making helpful and encouraging comments and offering the Library many interesting second-hand books which could be acquired from him for very moderate sums.

From 1984 to 1986, the Society was preoccupied with the situation whereby the National Library had remained under the control of the Department of Education while the National Museum had been transferred to the Department of the Taoiseach. The Library had been under the control of the Department of Education since 1924 and it was generally perceived that this department's attitude to the Library during its stewardship was one of, at best, benign neglect – it was plainly more concerned with the needs of first, second and third level education rather than with those of the State's cultural institutions under its care. At the Society's AGM of 1986 J.W. de Courcy, in the course of a speech proposing a motion to the effect that the Library should be placed under the aegis of the Department of the Taoiseach, said that "it was appropriate that this important repository of Irish culture should be placed under the care of the most important person in the country". The Library was eventually transferred to the Department of the Taoiseach in 1986, remaining with that department until, in 1991, a separate Department of Arts and Culture was established. In 2005, the Library became a semi-State institution under the provisions of the National Cultural Institutions Act, 1997.

In this period it was regrettable that the Society's membership continued to decline, at the rate of about thirty members per annum. On a more positive note, however, in June 1986 the Society organised the first summer tour for its members to libraries, historic buildings and other sites throughout Ireland. This visit was to the King's Inns in Dublin. The visiting Society members were greeted by Mr Justice Niall McCarthy and members of the Benchers of the King's Inns, and a reception was held. The Librarian of the King's Inns, Jonathan Armstrong, gave a tour of the library, while Maurice Craig gave a talk on the architecture and decoration of the magnificent Dining Hall. During the summer of the following year, a tour took place to the Bolton Library (Cashel Diocesan Library) and to Holycross Abbey, where the Chairman of the Society, Henry Wheeler, gave a talk. In the summer of 1988, the Society visited Kilkenny-Ossory Diocesan Library, Kilkenny Castle and St Canice's Cathedral. The author Hubert Butler spoke to the group at the cathedral.

During 1986 and 1987, the Society received the large bequest of £50,000 from the estate of Wanda Petronella Brown. Mrs Brown was the wife of J. Barry Brown, book collector, solicitor and sometime County Registrar for Kildare (whose brother was Fr Stephen Brown SJ, the bibliographer).

This splendid gift came to the Society entirely through the good offices of Patrick Henchy. Barry Brown, through his frequent visits to the Library, had become a good friend of Henchy.

Also in 1986 the Society received a bequest from E. Hilda Allberry, a member of the Executive Committee during the early years. She and her family were the publishers of *The Irish Builder and Engineer*. This magazine is an important source of Irish architectural history, especially for the nineteenth century. The National Library of Ireland featured in more than one article in the *Builder*. Much as she appreciated the magnificence of the Kildare Street building from the viewpoint of architectural history, it appeared to her that a new purpose-built library, on another site, was urgently required in order that the National Library should fulfil its functions adequately.

In November 1986 the Society published a memoir by Patrick Henchy in which he detailed his experiences of the Library during his time on the staff, from his appointment as an Assistant Librarian in 1941 to his years as Director. It was based on a lecture given to the Society during the previous year, and a copy was sent to all members. The launching ceremony, by Ted Nealon TD, Minister of State at the Department of the Taoiseach, took place in the National Gallery of Ireland. The publication contained several photographs and on the front cover there was a reproduction of a painting by Thomas Ryan, President of the Royal Hibernian Academy, depicting the Library's Reading Room as it was in 1962. Peter Tynan O'Mahony, a former *Irish Times* journalist, sometime editor of *O'Mahony News: Newsletter of the O'Mahony Record Society* and a member of the Executive Committee for years, was responsible for editing and designing this monograph. He was also editor and designer of two subsequent Society publications. A foreword in Irish was contributed by Seán Ó Lúing, the historical biographer and Stiúrthóir of An Roinn Aistriúcháin in Dáil Éireann, who was a good friend to the Society

Two years later, in 1988, the Society published another monograph, an account of the career of Edward MacLysaght, first Chief Herald of Ireland and Keeper of Manuscripts at the Library. It was compiled by Charles Lysaght – lawyer, diplomat and biographer, and a kinsman of Dr MacLysaght. The cover showed a reproduction of a portrait sketch of MacLysaght, again by Thomas Ryan.

At the Society's inaugural meeting (1969): (from left) Desmond Clarke, Professor Patrick Lynch, Dr Patrick Henchy, Senator Michael Yeats and Capt. Tadhg McGlinchey.

Kieran Hickey's *Portrait of a Library* (1976) being filmed in the Library's front hall.

Seán Ó Lúing speaking at the grave of Douglas Hyde, near Frenchpark, Co. Roscommon, on the Society's annual outing in 1993. His audience includes: (from left) Monica Henchy, Shiela de Courcy and Professor Seán de Courcy.

Presenting *Writers, Raconteurs and Notable Feminists* to President Mary Robinson in July 1994: (from left) Dr Patricia Donlon, President Robinson, Andrée Sheehy Skeffington and Alf Mac Lochlainn.

At Strokestown House, on the Society's annual outing in 1993: (from left) Dermot Blunden, Seán Ó Lúing and Dónall Ó Luanaigh

At the grave of Wolfe Tone, at Bodenstown, Co. Kildare on the Society's annual outing in 1998: (from left) Col. Con Costello, Dr Daire Keogh and Gerard Lyne.

Nóra Ní Shúilliobháin,
Honorary Treasurer, 1973–1990

Dr Margaret MacCurtain OP,
Chairman of the Society, 1996–2000.

Sketches by Brian Lalor, on the Society's annual outing in 2004: (clockwise, from top left) The Ladies; Clonfert Cathedral; Ormond Tower, Roscrea; and Birr Telescope.

Members of the Society outside the Northern Ireland Assembly building at Stormont, near Belfast, on the annual outing in 2005: (from left) Colette O'Daly, Gerard Long, Sandra McDermott, Séamus Ó Maitiú and Ciara Kerrigan.

Thomas Pakenham addressing the Society's members in Tullynally Castle on the annual outing in 2006.

Members of the Society in Clonmacnoise, Co. Offaly, on the annual outing in 2006: (sitting, from left) Máire Mac Conghail, Mary Ó Luanaigh, Colette O'Daly, Muriel McCarthy; (standing, from left) Ciara Kerrigan, Gerard Long, Anthony Behan, Dónall Ó Luanaigh and Sandra McDermott.

At the launch of the *Festschrift* for Dónall Ó Luanaigh in the National Library in 2007: the editor, Felix M. Larkin (left), with the honorand.

At the O'Meara lecture in 2008, Mrs Odile O'Meara and her family with the lecturer, Professor Eamon Duffy (second from left), Mr Justice Peter Kelly (who responded to Professor Duffy's lecture, far left) and Aongus Ó hAonghusa (Director of the National Library, far right)

Gerard Lyne reading from the poems of Francis Ledwidge outside the Ledwidge Museum in Slane, Co. Meath, on the Society's annual outing in 2009. On the left is the Society's Chairman, Fr J. Anthony Gaughan.

CHAPTER 3: 1989–2003

Early in 1989 Patricia Donlon succeeded Michael Hewson as Director of the Library. She had previously been Keeper of Western Collections at the Chester Beatty Library and had earlier been Deputy Librarian of the Royal Irish Academy. She was the first Director to be appointed by open competition. The post had been filled previously by internal promotion. The first head of the National Library in 1877, William Archer, had previously been Librarian of the Royal Dublin Society.

Soon after her arrival in the Library, Dr Donlon attended a meeting of the Executive Committee at which she expressed her appreciation of the work of the Society and looked forward to working with the Committee for the greater good of the Library, its staff and collections. She was later to lecture to the Society on her plans for the development of the Library.

However, this was a difficult period for the Library because of the need at the time for tight control of public expenditure. An embargo on appointments and promotions in the public service, coupled with a number of early retirements, had forced the Library to suspend evening and Saturday openings. At the Society's AGM in April 1989 a motion was carried which called on the Taoiseach, as a matter of urgency, to fill vacancies on the staff of the Library in order that it could revert to normal opening hours and otherwise restore the level of its services to Irish scholarship and to the international community of scholars.

One of the early lecturers to the Society during the 1970s had been Maurice B. Line, then on the senior staff of the British Library. Line went on to become an internationally recognised consultant on the preparation of strategic plans for national and academic libraries. In 1989 the Council of Trustees of the National Library decided to request Dr Line to survey the Library and to advise on the preparation of a strategic plan. Immediate access to funding being very scarce in the Library just then, the Society was happy to accede to the Director's request to cover the cost of Line's initial visit to Dublin.

The very popular summer tours organised by the Society continued. In 1989 the Society visited St Patrick's College Maynooth, where a tour of the library and the college's Scientific Museum took place. Henry Wheeler gave a guided tour of Maynooth Castle, while the group also visited Carton House and viewed its beautiful ceilings. Two years later, the Society had a memorable outing to the Pearse Museum at St Enda's, Rathfarnham, where the curator, Pat Cooke, received the party. On the same day, there was a visit to Rathfarnham Castle, where Maurice Craig spoke on the history of the building and its recent restoration by the Office of Public Works.

During 1990 the Society presented the Library with a microfilm camera and also hosted a reception to launch an exhibition based on Liam O'Leary's archive on the history of the cinema, which he had recently donated to the Library.

In June 1991 Dónall Ó Luanaigh resigned as Honorary Secretary and was succeeded by Gerard Lyne. Membership of the Society had fallen a little further and now stood at 400, and the new Secretary set out to change this. A new scheme of life membership of the Society at a fee of £100, now €126, was instituted. Lyne also introduced the practice of printing large-size illustrated posters to announce individual lectures. These were distributed to Dublin public library branches and other public places from this time onwards. A new publicity brochure for the Society, with application form, appeared in 1992. There was a foreword from the Director, endorsing the Society. The brochure contained a colour photograph of the Library as it appeared during the years when readers such as Arthur Griffith, James Joyce, Patrick Pearse and Francis and Hanna Sheehy Skeffington were familiar figures in the Reading Room. Between 1992 and 1995, 10,000 copies of this brochure were distributed.

During the summer of 1992 the Society organised a tour to Carriglass Manor, Co. Longford, which had been the home of Lord Chief Justice Lefroy, who some say was the model for Mr D'Arcy in Jane Austen's novel *Pride and Prejudice*. The Society also visited Tullynally, Co. Westmeath, the family seat of the Earls of Longford.

Henry Wheeler resigned as Chairman in the summer of 1992, to be succeeded by J.W. (Seán) de Courcy, Professor of Civil Engineering at UCD, and the author of *The Liffey in Dublin* (1996). De Courcy had been active on the Executive Committee of the Society in its very early days. Honorary membership of the Society was conferred on the outgoing Chairman and also on the Director, Dr Donlon, and on Nóra Ní Shúilliobháin (who had resigned as Honorary Treasurer in 1990, having served in that office since 1973). Ní Shúilliobháin was succeeded as Treasurer by Dermot Blunden, who held an administrative post with Arthur Guinness Ltd and was also an enthusiastic genealogist. He was also both Secretary and Treasurer of the Ireland Branch of the Irish Genealogical Research Society.

Many of the lectures given to the Society during the 1980s and early 1990s were recorded through the kindness and consideration of Brian Lynch, archivist and historian of RTÉ. Mr Lynch has also lectured to the Society a number of times on subjects relating to broadcasting.

From this period, at the request of the Director, the Society provided funding for several years for a Christmas party hosted by the Council of Trustees for Library staff. The Society also gave financial assistance on more than one occasion to a football club set up by younger staff members in order to compete in civil service soccer leagues.

During 1993 the Society made a small presentation to its founder and patron, Patrick Henchy, to mark his eightieth birthday. In June, the Society's tour took place to Strokestown House and Famine Museum and to Clonalis, Co. Roscommon, home of the O'Conor Don family. On the same day, Seán Ó Lúing gave an address on behalf of the Society at the grave of Douglas Hyde near Frenchpark, Co. Roscommon, and laid a wreath to commemorate the centenary of the foundation of Conradh na Gaeilge. Among the Life Members of the Society who joined in 1993 were: Mary Banotti MEP; Peter Cassells, General Secretary of ICTU; and Senator Maurice Manning. Kieran Hickey, the film director who had directed the 1976 film *Portrait of a Library*, died in 1993. He had been a good friend of the Society from its foundation.

In December 1993, at the request of the Director, the Society provided funding of £3,000 for the publication of a catalogue of the Library's Brocas Collection of original drawings, compiled by Patricia Butler. Shortly afterwards, in February 1994, the Society gave a donation of £500 to the Linen Hall Library in Belfast as a gesture of goodwill and solidarity following a fire-bomb attack on the library. In 1994 the Society also made a donation to the newly founded Cardinal Ó Fiaich Memorial Library in Armagh.

On 13 July 1994 Her Excellency, the President of Ireland, Mary Robinson, was presented with a copy of the Society's most recent publication at a ceremony held in Áras an Uachtaráin. The publication,

Writers, Raconteurs and Notable feminists, consisted of two essays by Alf Mac Lochlainn and Andrée Sheehy Skeffington. Designed and edited by Peter Tynan O'Mahony, the foreword was by Dónall Ó Luanaigh, the former Honorary Secretary of the Society.

Early in 1995 honorary membership of the Society was conferred on Jean Kennedy Smith, then United States Ambassador to Ireland.

At the AGM of the Society in 1995, a motion was carried welcoming the decision of the Minister for Arts and Culture to confer semi-State status on the National Library, with hopes that this would entail provision of adequate funding for the Library to discharge its functions properly. At the request of the Executive Committee, one of its members, Harold O'Sullivan, former President of the Irish Congress of Trade Unions, and a prominent local historian, prepared a memorandum on the implications for the Library of becoming a semi-State institution. A copy of this memorandum was sent to the Director of the Library. As Dr O'Sullivan had served on the board of more than one State-sponsored body, he wrote from experience. The urgency of this question, however, receded with the change of government in 1997, and implementation of the National Cultural Institutions Act 1997 (which provided for the change in the structure of the Library from a body within the civil service to a semi-State body) was deferred. The Act was finally implemented in 2005. The Library became a semi-State body under the supervision of a board whose members are appointed by the Minister for Arts, Sport and Tourism – a structure which the Society had recommended as far back as 1973.

Professor de Courcy resigned as Chairman of the Executive Committee in 1996 and was succeeded by Margaret Mac Curtain OP, the well-known UCD historian. In 1997 the Society suffered a sad loss with the death of Dermot Blunden, the Honorary Treasurer. Although he died following a long illness, he had continued to faithfully discharge his duties as Treasurer almost up to the very end. As a small token of the Society's appreciation of his work, honorary membership of the Society was conferred on his wife, Bernadette, who continues to support Society events. He was succeeded as Treasurer by Ciárán Ó hÓgartaigh, then of Dublin City University and subsequently Professor of Accountancy in UCD.

In 1997 the Society organised a special lecture in memory of Thomas P. O'Neill, whose death had occurred during the previous year. From Co. Carlow, Tom O'Neill (as he was always known in the Library) began his career on the professional staff of the Library during the 1940s after graduating in history from UCD. He published a study of James Fintan Lalor in Irish in 1962 (an English translation of this book, by John T. Goulding, appeared in 2003). In 1963 he obtained special leave from the Library in order to undertake the authorised biography of President de Valera. This work, with the Earl of Longford as co-author, was published in 1970. O'Neill went on to join the staff of the Department of Modern Irish History in University College Galway, later becoming Professor of Modern Irish History there. On his retirement from this post, he returned to live in Dublin and became an active member of the Society's Executive Committee. He also lectured to the Society. The Thomas P. O'Neill memorial lecture was given by Thomas Bartlett on the subject of Irish Catholics during the eighteenth century.

The Society's summer tour in 1997 was to the former home of Maria Edgeworth at Edgeworthstown, Co. Longford, and to the Franciscan Abbey at Multyfarnham, Co. Westmeath.

Dr Donlon retired as Director of the Library for health reasons early in 1997. As an interim measure, Seán Cromien, formerly Secretary General of the Department of Finance, was appointed by the Council of Trustees as Acting Director. Later in the year, Brendan O Donoghue, formerly Secretary General of the Department of the Environment, became Director. O Donoghue had been a regular reader in the Library in the course of his research over many years on the history of Irish civil engineering which has borne fruit in the publication of two books by him on this subject – one a study of the Leahy family of engineers 1780–1888, the other a biographical dictionary of the Irish county surveyors 1834–1944. At the time of Dr Donlon's retirement, the Executive Committee noted the discrepancy between the salary attached to the Director's post and the salaries of the heads of other Irish academic libraries, the latter often considerably in excess of the Director's salary.

In July 1998 Gerard Lyne resigned as Honorary Secretary, to be succeeded by Gerard Long, Assistant Keeper of Printed Books. A great bibliophile, Long has been a strong supporter of the Society for many years and regularly attends the Society's functions and maintains contact with members both young and not so young. Here he follows a tradition set by his late father, Seán Ó Lúing. In recent years he has been a member of the Board of the Library representing the staff. He was succeeded as Secretary by Colette O'Flaherty,

Sandra McDermott and Ciara Kerrigan, all of them members of the Library's librarian or archivist staff. The present Secretary, Roger Courtney, is a member of the staff of the Financial Department of the Library.

On Sunday 12 December 1999, after Divine Service, the Society was allowed to plant a silver birch tree in the churchyard of Rathmichael Parish Church, Co. Dublin, in memory of Sir John Ainsworth, Bart., and his wife, Anita Lady Ainsworth. Sir John Francis Ainsworth was Inspector of Manuscripts with the Irish Manuscripts Commission and with the National Library from the mid-1940s until his death in 1981. In his capacity as inspector, he prepared hundreds of reports on estate archives in private possession and was responsible for the subsequent acquisition of many of these vast collections by the Library. Educated at Eton and at Trinity College Cambridge, he was the editor of *The Inchiquin Papers* (Dublin, 1961) and also edited the periodical *Analecta Hibernica* for a number of years. The idea of planting a tree in their memory came about because of Lady Ainsworth's interest in gardening.

In the year 2000, Dr Mac Curtain resigned from the chair of the Society and was succeeded by the present Chairman, Fr J. Anthony Gaughan PP, biographer and historian. Fr Gaughan was Chairman of PEN in Ireland and one of the founders of Listowel Writers' Week. As Chairman of the Executive Committee of the Society, Fr Gaughan was appointed to the new Library Board's statutory Readers Advisory Committee in 2006, a welcome recognition of the Society's place in the life and development of the Library.

During 2000, honorary membership of the Society was conferred on Michael, Gráinne and Anne Yeats in recognition of the generosity of the Yeats family in donating the papers of William Butler Yeats to the National Library.

Patrick Henchy, the founder and patron of the Society, died on 6 May 2001. His wife Monica, who was on the staff of the Library of Trinity College Dublin, has been an active member of the Executive Committee for a number of years and has lectured to the Society on the history of the Irish Colleges in Spain. Nóra Ní Shúilliobháin, the long-time Honorary Treasurer of the Society, also died in 2001. The Kerry Historical Society's Dublin Branch organises an annual lecture in her memory which the Library is happy to host.

After many years of devoted service on the Executive Committee, Veronica McEvatt resigned in 2001. The Society's annual outing that year took place to the Hunt Museum in Limerick.

In 2002 the Director of the Library, Brendan O Donoghue, suggested to the Executive Committee that a consultant might be engaged to review the role of the Society. However, the Executive Committee decided, after a discussion, not to adopt this suggestion. Just a few years earlier, the then Chairman, Margaret Mac Curtain, had suggested that there was a need to re-define the role of the Society and had asked: "Was [its] main function to sponsor lectures…?" It will be recalled that uncertainty about the exact role of the Society had first come to light after Patrick Henchy resigned as Director of the Library in 1976, and this is still a topic of debate.

Felix M. Larkin, a senior public servant and historian who has played a major role in the Society in recent years, first joined the Executive Committee in 2002. In the following year he was appointed Honorary Treasurer in succession to Ciarán Ó hÓgartaigh and became Vice-Chairman in 2007. His efforts, especially in conjunction with Sandra McDermott during her time as Honorary Secretary, have given the Society a new lease of life, despite the ongoing uncertainly about what its role should be. A new membership brochure was produced in 2003, and in the following years membership numbers gradually increased to their current level of about 550.

In the summer of 2003, the Society's outing took place to Stradbally Hall and to Emo Court, both in Co. Laois. Anthony J. Hughes, who had been for many years Chairman of the Council of Trustees was conferred with Honorary Membership of the Society in 2003. At the same time, the following former members of the Council of Trustees were also conferred with Honorary Membership: Brian Murphy (former Chairman of the Office of Public Works), Mary J.P. Scannell and John Turpin.

Brendan O Donoghue retired as Director of the Library in 2003. His tenure had seen an enormous improvement in the Library's circumstances and in staff morale, developments much welcomed by the Society. Aongus Ó hAonghusa, who had previously been Keeper of Administration in the Library, was appointed Acting Director and became Director in 2005. Mr Ó hAonghusa resigned from the post of Director in January 2010 in order to return to the civil service.

CHAPTER 4: 2004–2010

In 2004 the splendid exhibition and outreach area in the refurbished former National College of Art building became available to the Library. Since then, with the kind permission of the Board of the Library, the Society's lectures and film shows have taken place in the fine lecture theatre in this building. The Library's acquisition of the College of Art premises represents the realisation of a suggestion first made by the Executive Committee of the Society in 1973 to John Bruton. A further suggestion made by the Society on that occasion, that the Library should become a semi-State body, was implemented in the following year when the provisions of the National Cultural Institutions Act, 1997 relating to the National Library were finally brought into force.

Also in 2004 the Society published Randal Sadleir's memoir of his father, Thomas Ulick Sadleir. The Deputy Ulster King of Arms, Thomas Sadleir oversaw the transfer of the Office of the Ulster King of Arms to the Irish State when it became the Genealogical Office/Office of Arms. The memoir, which was launched in the Heraldic Museum in June 2004, was jointly funded by the National Library and by the Society.

The Society's summer outing in 2004 took place to Damer House, Roscrea, Birr Castle and Clonfert Cathedral.

In 2005 the Director of the Library requested the Society to take on the organisation of a memorial lecture series in honour of the late John J. O'Meara of UCD, classicist and educationalist. These lectures were made possible by a generous endowment from Professor O'Meara's family. O'Meara, who died in 2003, was an active member of the National Library of Ireland Society for many years and had served on its Executive Committee. It is therefore fitting that the Society should host the lecture series which his family has funded. A list of the lectures given to date is given in Appendix 3. As well as donating funds to set up this lecture series, Professor O'Meara's family presented his archive to the National Library.

The Society's summer outing in 2005 was to the Northern Ireland Assembly building at Stormont, to the birthplace of C.S. Lewis in Belfast and to St Mark's Church, Dundela (which contains a stained-glass window commemorating Lewis' family). Hillsborough Castle, Co. Down, was also visited on this occasion. The participants will never forget the moment when the current Chairman of the Society, Fr J. Anthony Gaughan, rose to say grace before lunch in the main dining room in Stormont, a sanctum more usually associated with another clergyman!

In 2005 the Society undertook its most ambitious publication. This was a commemorative volume for Dónall Ó Luanaigh on his retirement from the post of Keeper of Collections in the Library. The Society arranged financial assistance for this publication from the National Library itself, the American Conference of Irish Historians and a number of generous anonymous donors, as well as contributing funding from the Society's own resources. The *Festschrift* was edited by Felix M. Larkin, Vice-Chairman of the Society, and was published in 2007 by Four Courts Press in association with the Society. Consisting of 367 pages and thirteen photographic and line drawing illustrations, it contains nineteen essays and nine poems (including five short poems by Seamus Heaney, translated from the Irish). Twelve of the essays are based on lectures previously given to the Society. As regards historical subjects, these range from early medieval to contemporary Ireland.

While most of the thirty-one contributors are from the island of Ireland, one contributor is from the United Kingdom, one from the United States of America, a third teaches at the Université de la Sorbonne Nouvelle in Paris and a fourth is retired from the University of Edinburgh. The editor has gratefully acknowledged the patience and unfailing assistance of the late Michael Adams of Four Courts Press in seeing the volume through the press and also the help of Noel Kissane, formerly Keeper of Manuscripts in the Library, in copy-editing the volume. James McGuire, Managing Editor of the Royal Irish Academy's *Dictionary of Irish Biography*, launched the book at a reception hosted by the National Library on 8 November 2007. Although commemorative volumes of this kind are generally compiled for academics only, two other such volumes dedicated to Irish librarians have appeared in recent years. These honour respectively the late Mary P. (Paul) Pollard, who was Keeper of Early Printed Books in the Library of Trinity College Dublin, and Mary Kelleher, until recently Librarian of the Royal Dublin Society.

The annual outing of the Society in the summer of 2006 took place to Tullynally Castle, where the group was received by its owner, the distinguished historian, Thomas Pakenham. The historical sites of Clonmacnoise, Co. Offaly and Fore Abbey, Co. Westmeath, were also visited on this occasion.

The summer tour of 2007 took place to Castleward, Co. Down. On the same day, the Society visited Down Cathedral in Downpatrick, where a talk was given by Gordon Wheeler, formerly of the Library of the Queen's University Belfast. Finally, the party viewed a small church near Rathfriland, Co. Down, which is associated with the Rev. Patrick Brontë, father of Anne, Emily and Charlotte Brontë. Here a talk was given by local historian Jason Diamond.

On the Society's summer tour in 2009, the members visited Beaulieu House and gardens near Drogheda, the Francis Ledwidge Museum in Slane, Co. Meath, and Larchill Arcadian Garden, a *ferme ornée* dating from the seventeenth century.

Another significant event in 2009 was the presentation, through the agency of the Society, of a rare seventeenth-century atlas to the Library by Annraí Ó Braonáin and his wife, Donla Uí Bhraonáin. The atlas consists of Irish maps from Volume V of Joan Blaeu's *Atlas Novus*, published in Amsterdam in 1654. Ó Braonáin has been a faithful member of the Executive Committee of the Society for some years now. Moreover, as part of the Society's Christmas event in December 2009, Nicholas Robinson (husband of former President Mary Robinson, and himself a cartoonist of note) launched a new book by Felix M. Larkin, Vice-Chairman of the Society, about the Shemus cartoons in the *Freeman's Journal*. The Library had acquired over 250 original drawings of the Shemus cartoons in 2006, with the assistance and on the recommendation of Mr Larkin. His book, entitled *Terror and Discord*, was published by A&A Farmar in association with the National Library of Ireland.

Larkin, formerly Honorary Treasurer, had become Vice-Chairman of the Society in 2007. He succeeded Muriel McCarthy, the long-serving Librarian of Marsh's Library. Dr McCarthy's involvement with and commitment to the Society over many years continued the tradition of support for the Society from other Dublin libraries which has been a feature of its history from the beginning. Felix Larkin was succeeded as Treasurer by Ian d'Alton, also a senior public servant and historian.

Late in 2008, in response to the then current grave crisis in the public finances, the government announced plans in the Budget to merge the National Library with the National Archives and the Irish Manuscripts Commission. Though subsequent events might appear to have deflected attention from these plans to more urgent matters, at the time of writing it is understood that arrangements for the merger are in train. In any event, the present national financial stringency will undoubtedly result in serious difficulties for the Library's own plans for the future, particularly with regard to the provision of adequate storage space and staffing levels. Indeed, the maintenance of services at their present level may even to be put at risk. In such difficult times as these, it would appear that the Library's need for the external support of the Society may well be greater than ever before. As Patricia Donlon wrote in the conclusion to her foreword to the Society's brochure in 1992, "Where would we be without our friends?"

Friends, indeed – and whatever the future may hold, it is unlikely that it will ever be possible to improve on the encomium bestowed by the *Irish Times* on the Society in 1976 which is quoted as the epigraph to the introduction to this history. That encomium is a fitting tribute to all who have been associated with the Society in the first forty years of its existence.

Appendix 1

Lectures, literary readings, and film shows organised by the
National Library of Ireland Society in Dublin since its foundation in 1969

NOTE: Those marked * have been published in Felix M. Larkin (ed.), *Librarians, Poets and Scholars: a Festschrift for Dónall Ó Luanaigh* (Dublin, 2007)

1970
Kenneth W. Humphreys
(International library consultant)
National libraries in general, with special reference to the National Library of Ireland

1971
Patrick Henchy
(Director, National Library of Ireland)
The National Library of Ireland: its history and collections
"Faithful Departed", a film directed by Kieran Hickey and based on the Lawrence Photographic Collection in the National Library of Ireland, was shown after this lecture

J. Gerard Slevin
(Chief Herald of Ireland)
The science and art of heraldry

J. Gerard Slevin
(Chief Herald of Ireland)
Genealogical research

1972
Edward MacLysaght
(Chairman, Irish Manuscripts Commission)
Collecting manuscripts [for the National Library of Ireland]

George Morrison
Film archives

"The Light of Other Days", a film directed by Kieran Hickey and based on the Lawrence Photographic Collection in the National Library of Ireland

Lord Wolfenden
From my Bloomsbury window: experiences and observations as Director of the British Museum

J.H. Andrews
Irish maps and cartographers

1973
Michael Hewson
(Keeper, National Library of Ireland)
Prints and Drawings in the National Library of Ireland

Maurice J. Craig
Irish bookbindings

David Jenkins
(Librarian, National Library of Wales)
The National Library of Wales

1974
Short films, directed by Kieran Hickey, dealing with Dion Boucicault, James Joyce and Jonathan Swift

Denis Roberts
(Librarian, National Library of Scotland)
The National Library of Scotland

1975
"For the Strength of the Hills", a film
dealing with the collection of the
Genealogical Society of Latter Day
Saints at Salt Lake City, Utah, USA

Kevin B. Nowlan
*Daniel O'Connell's place in Irish
nationalism*

Kevin B. Nowlan (*in the Chair*)
Symposium on newspapers as a source
of Irish history

1976
Maurice B. Line
(British Library)
The British Library

"Portrait of a Library", a film dealing
with the National Library of Ireland,
directed by Kieran Hickey

Mairéad MacParland (Conservator,
National Gallery of Ireland) & Alf
Mac Lochlainn (Director, National
Library of Ireland)
*Paper and the history of papermaking
in Ireland*

1977
Eddie Chandler
(Historian of Irish photography)
The magic lantern
Illustrated by items from the
lantern-slide collection of the
National Library of Ireland

Patrick Henchy
(Director, Chester Beatty Library
and Gallery of Oriental Art)
*The Joly family and the National
Library of Ireland*
Published in the *Irish University
Review*, 7:2 (Autumn 1977)

1978
J. Gerard Slevin
(Chief Herald of Ireland)
Ex libris *in the National Library
of Ireland*
This lecture was based mainly on the
Sir Neville Wilkinson Collection and
the Chamney Collection of bookplates
in the Genealogical Office

Horst Ernestus
(City Librarian of Wuppertal, Germany)
Developments in German libraries

Michael Hewson
(Keeper of Printed Books, National
Library of Ireland)
*Caricatures in the collection of the
National Library of Ireland*

Michael O'Brien
(The O'Brien Press, Dublin)
The modern publishing revolution

1979
J.B. Malone
*Dublin street scenes as shown
in old bill-heads*

C.P. Hyland
(Antiquarian bookseller)
The antiquarian book trade

J.H. Andrews
Map makers and map readers: the case of the Ordnance Survey

1980
K. W. Nicholls
Irish genealogy – myth or reality?

F. E. Dixon
Postcards as sources of information
Illustrated from the collection of postcards which Mr Dixon had presented to the National Library of Ireland

Nessa Ní Shéaghdha
(Dublin Institute of Advanced Studies, School of Celtic Studies)
Scribes, patrons, collectors: the history of Irish language manuscripts

Henry J. Heaney
(Librarian of the University of Glasgow)
Visitors' books – an account of some tours of Ireland

1981
Mary Buckley
Thomas Davis, with particular reference to sources for the story of his life and work which are available in the National Library of Ireland

Dónall Ó Luanaigh
(Keeper, Department of Manuscripts, National Library of Ireland)
Manuscript journals in the National Library of Ireland of visitors to France during the eighteenth and nineteenth centuries

Gerard Lyne
(Assistant Keeper, Department of Manuscripts, National Library of Ireland)
Social life in the papers of the O'Connell family of Derrynane, Co. Kerry

J.W. de Courcy
Alexander Nimmo, engineer, and his work in Ireland

1982
Edward More O'Ferrall
Lord Edward FitzGerald (including a medical report on the last thirty-six hours of his life)

Gearóid Denvir
Pádraic Ó Conaire

1983
R.V. Comerford
Charles Kickham and some hidden Irelands

Noel Hughes
(Librarian of An Foras Forbartha)
Irish engineering, 1760-1960: literature in the Library of the Institute of Engineers of Ireland

Mark Bence-Jones
Irish houses

1984
"The Chester Beatty Library, where East meets West", a film directed by Kieran Hickey

J.B. Lyons
Oliver St John Gogarty

Maurice R. O'Connell
Daniel O'Connell and Young Ireland

Benedict Kiely
Peadar O'Donnell: a tribute
Mr O'Donnell was present
at this lecture

1985
Brendan Kennelly
A reading of his work, including
Cromwell, a dramatic poem

Mary P. (Paul) Pollard
(Keeper of Early Printed Books,
TCD Library)
*The supply of books in
eighteenth-century Dublin*

Patrick Henchy
(formerly Director,
National Library of Ireland)
*The National Library of Ireland
1941-1976: a look back*
Published by the Society in 1986

Alf Mac Lochlainn
(Librarian of University College
Galway and formerly Director,
National Library of Ireland)
*"Those young men…": contemporaries
of James Joyce*
Published by the Society in 1994

1986
Christopher N. Murray
*James Sheridan Knowles: dramatist
and actor-manager*

Micheline Kerney-Walsh
*Gleanings from Continental manuscripts:
the career in Spain of Donal O'Sullivan
Beare*

Robert G. Hogan
*Joseph Holloway: diarist
and theatre-goer*

1987
Seamus Heaney
A reading of his work

Gréagóir Ó Dúill
Sir Samuel Ferguson

John M. Gilmartin
James Barry, artist

Liam O'Leary
Tradition in the Irish cinema

Charles E. Lysaght
*Edward Mac Lysaght, first Chief
Herald of Ireland and Keeper of
Manuscripts in the National Library
of Ireland*
Published by the Society in 1988

Pádraig Ó Snodaigh
*The life and works of Joseph Mary
Plunkett*
With a reading of Plunkett's poetry
by Pádraig Mac Cuaig

1988
"Ireland, a writers' island", a film
directed by Vincent Corcoran
Introduced by Mr Corcoran

John B. O'Brien
*The role of the Irish in Australian society
during the nineteenth and twentieth
centuries*

Rev. Liam Swords
*The Irish Colleges in Paris during
the French Revolution*

Henry A. Wheeler
*Dublin City churches of the Church
of Ireland*

1989
Kevin Whelan
*A new interpretation of the 1798
Rebellion in Co. Wexford*

Eavan Boland
A reading of her work

"Faithful Departed" and "The Dead",
films directed by Kieran Hickey
and John Huston respectively
Both films were introduced
by Mr Hickey

Andrée Sheehy Skeffington
Some Irish women I have known
Published by the Society in 1994

Muiris Mac Conghail
An illustrated account of the making of
his films about the Blasket Islands and
the Aran Islands

Jennifer Johnston
A reading of her work

1990
Neil Jordan
An illustrated review of his films

Patricia Donlon
(Director, National Library of Ireland)
*The National Library of Ireland: plans
for the future*

Gerard Long
(Assistant Keeper, National Library
of Ireland)
*The foundation of the National Library
of Ireland in 1877: the political and
cultural background*

Frederick O'Dwyer
(Architectural historian)
*The National Library and the National
Museum: the design and construction
of the buildings*

Edward McParland
(Architectural historian)
Irish and European library buildings

"A Spendthrift of Genius", a film about
the life of Oscar Wilde directed by
Seán Ó Mórdha
Introduced by Mr Ó Mórdha

Maurice B. Line
(International library consultant)
Have national libraries a future?

Alan Marchbank
(Director of Public Services, National
Library of Scotland)
The National Library of Scotland today

Dermot McGuinne
Printing types in the Irish character

1991
Donal F. Begley
(Chief Herald of Ireland)
*Heraldry in the Ormond deed collection
in the National Library of Ireland*

Eilís Ní Dhuibhne
(Curator, Department of Prints and
Drawings, National Library of Ireland)
*"Look here upon this picture…": the
cartoonists' image of Charles Stewart
Parnell, his supporters and opponents,
1877-1891*

"At the Cinema Palace", a film directed
by Donald Taylor Black about the life
and work of Liam O'Leary

James Plunkett
Remembrance of things past

Tim Pat Coogan
*Flawed title deeds: an analysis
of political myths in Ireland*

1992
Joseph J. Lee
Interpreting modern Irish history

Nuala Ní Dhomhnaill
*Epiphanies: the way of poetic
consciousness*

Richard Kearney
*Region, nation, federation: Ireland's
European wager*

John McGahern
The solitary reader

John Banville
A reading from his novel *Ghosts*

Nuala O'Faolain leads a discussion
on "Writing for a Living"

Anthony Clare
*Psychological reflections on Irish
Catholicism*

1993
Seamus Deane
Swift: virtue and travel

Thomas P. O'Neill
The 1916 Proclamation

Tom McIntyre
Writer and roots

Proinsias MacAonghusa
(Uachtarán, Conradh na Gaeilge)
*Conradh na Gaeilge: léacht dá-theangach
fén gConradh i láthair na h-uaire agus
amach anseo*

J.P. Donleavy
The world of the writer

1994
Margaret Mac Curtain OP
*The writing and publishing of the
history of women in Ireland*

Cormac Ó Gráda
*The Famine in Dublin in folklore
and song*

Lorna Reynolds
Kate O'Brien: artist and feminist

Michael Laffan
*Purists and pragmatists: the Sinn Féin
party and the Treaty split, 1921-1922*

Owen Dudley Edwards
Sir Arthur Conan Doyle and Ireland

1995
Gemma Hussey
*The maelstrom in the middle:
government and the need for
electoral reform*

Harry Bradshaw
Captain Francis O'Neill, Chicago police chief and collector of Irish traditional music

George Huxley
Latent treasures: some rare books in the Library of the Royal Irish Academy

Roy Foster
A continual apology: W.B. Yeats, Irish history and the function of biography

Eileen Battersby
Reviews, responsibility, ethics and politics

Brendan Bradshaw
The history of "these islands"

Marina Carr
"That unrepeatable road": writers who have influenced me

1996
Tom Garvin
"Tell me a story…": mythological thinking in Irish political life

Muriel McCarthy
(Librarian, Archbishop Marsh's Library)
Simony, sacrilege and perjury: Archbishop Marsh and his Library

Brian Lynch
(Archivist, RTÉ)
Women and the early broadcasting service

Ulick O'Connor
The Irish literary renaissance

Merlin Holland
Killing one bird with two stones: Dorian Gray and the downfall of Oscar Wilde

Thomas Kilroy
The contemporary Irish theatre

1997
Angela Bourke
The burning of Bridget Cleary: rumours, legends and documents

J.W. de Courcy
The Liffey and James Joyce: local comments from the sideline

Thomas Bartlett
Survival and revival: Irish Catholics in the eighteenth century
The Thomas P. O'Neill Lecture

Bishop James Kavanagh & James Larkin
"Big Jim" Larkin: his work and family

Angus Mitchell
The Casement papers: some new discoveries

Terry Eagleton
Yeats and poetic form

1998
Micheal O'Siadhail
A fragile jazz: a reading of his work

Declan Kiberd
From modern to post-modern: Joyce and Beckett

Maureen Murphy
Hope from the ocean: Irish servant girls in America

Rev. Leonard Boyle OP
(Vatican Librarian)
The history and treasures of the Vatican Library

Monica Henchy
* The Irish Colleges in Spain, 1592–1951

Brian Cosgrove
Joyce and some European precursors

1999
Hugh Shields
English, Irish and the making of traditional music

Brendan O Donoghue
(Director, National Library of Ireland)
* From grand juries to county councils: the importance of the Local Government (Ireland) Act of 1898

James S. Donnelly
The cult of the Blessed Virgin Mary in Ireland after the Second Vatican Council: the background to the "moving statues" of 1985

Monica McWilliams
The role of women in Northern Ireland politics

Bruce Arnold
Unravelling Swift: Jonathan Swift and his contemporaries

Marianne McDonald
Cool classics, Irish fire: Ancient Greek tragedy by modern Irish writers

Margaret Ó hÓgartaigh
Far from few: professional women in Ireland between 1880 and 1930

2000
Michael Longley
A paper screen
A reading to mark the publication of his book *The Weather in Japan*

Marie Coleman
The role of Piaras Béaslaí in the Irish Revolution, 1916-1923

Peter Harbison
Béranger's eighteenth-century views of Ireland

Robert Monks
The making of the film "Guests of the Nation"

Marie O'Neill
Grace Gifford Plunkett and Irish freedom

Alan Fletcher
Base bards and boisterous buffoons: the professional entertainers and early Gaelic Ireland

2001
Elaine Condon
Sketchbooks of Charles Rennie Mackintosh in the National Library of Ireland

Stephen Ball
(Assistant Keeper, Department of Manuscripts, National Library of Ireland)
Some aspects of the Clonbrock papers in the National Library of Ireland

Theo Dorgan
O'Malley's children: a review of his own poetry and that of his contemporaries

Brian Lynch
(Archivist, RTÉ)
Two lives in broadcasting: a centenary sketch of Maurice Gorham

Patrick Geoghegan
An act of power and corruption: the bicentennial debate
This lecture marked the bicentennial of the Act of Union of 1800

Éilís Ní Dhuibhne
(Assistant Keeper, National Library of Ireland)
Part-time: on being a librarian and a writer

2002
Randal Sadleir
Memories of the Office of Arms, 1933-1943
Published by the Society in 2004

Gerard Lyne
(Keeper of Manuscripts, National Library of Ireland)
A controversial land agent: William Steuart Trench and the Lansdowne estate in Co. Kerry, 1849-1872

Maria Luddy
The Women's History Project

Gabriel Fitzmaurice
A reading of his work

David Murphy
Dr Robert McDonnell (1828-1889): an Irish surgeon in the Crimea

Adrian Frazier
* George Moore, W.K. Magee and R. I. Best: how librarians and writers collaborate

2003
Síghle Bhreathnach-Lynch
* The search for national identity: expressions of Ireland's nationhood in bronze and stone

James McGuire
(Managing Editor, *The Dictionary of Irish Biography*)
The Dictionary of Irish Biography

Éilís Ní Bhrádaigh
Children's street games: a paradise lost

Maurice Harmon
Thomas Kinsella: a poet of many voices

Moya Cannon
A reading of her work

Ruan O'Donnell
The life and legacy of Robert Emmet

Niall Keogh
The Wicklow papers in the National Library of Ireland

Simon J. Potter
The Irish media and the British Empire

2004
Ian d'Alton
* Survival and adaptation? Cork Protestants in the nineteenth and twentieth centuries

Finola Kennedy
* Family change in Ireland

Louis Marcus
History in films: use or abuse?

Anthony Summers
*Conspiracy and the Kennedy
assassination. Not a mirage?*

Denis O'Driscoll
A reading of his work

Antoinette Quinn
*Patrick Kavanagh's "Collected Poems":
the centenary edition*

Diarmuid Whelan
* *A genetic echo: the life and thought of
Francis Sheehy Skeffington and Owen
Sheehy Skeffington*

David Murphy
*The Arctic Fox: the life of Sir Francis
Leopold McClintock, Polar explorer*

2005
Fergus Gillespie
(Chief Herald of Ireland)
* *Sons of Milesius: The Irish in Spain
in the Middle Ages*

Felix M. Larkin
* *Mrs Jellyby's daughter: Caroline Agnes
Gray and the "Freeman's Journal"*

"The Irish Question", a film in
the *March of Time* series, with an
introduction by Robert Monks

Breandán Ó Cathaoir
Charles Hart: Young Irelander abroad

A.P.W. Malcomson
*The Clements Project: the Clements
papers in the National Library of
Ireland*

Mr Justice Adrian Hardiman
* *"A gruesome case": James Joyce's Dublin
murder trial*

Dermot Bolger
My life in boxes

Claudia Kinmonth
*The narrative of the painting
"St Patrick's Day" by C.H. Cook*

2006
Deirdre McMahon
*An oral history of Irish Catholic
missionaries in India*

"Cradle of Genius", a film about the
Abbey Theatre directed by Paul Rotha,
with comments by Shivaun O'Casey
and Christopher N. Murray

Hilary Pyle
*Sadhbh Trínseach: what the National
Library notebooks reveal*

Ciarán Ó hÓgartaigh & Margaret
Ó hÓgartaigh
* *Teaching accounting in the eighteenth
century*

Claire Keegan
A reading of her work

L.P. Curtis Jr
*Images of eviction: "…and the walls
came tumbalin' down…" – the battering
ram and Irish evictions*
Published in *Éire-Ireland*, 42:3&4
(Fall/Winter 2007)

Brian Lynch
(Archivist, RTÉ)
*From wireless to web: Easter Week and
Irish broadcasting*

Anne Dolan
Killing and Bloody Sunday,
November 1920

2007
Rolf Loeber & Magda Loeber
Irish fiction in the English language,
1650-1900: a journey of discovery

Brian Lalor
"Take in your ink-stained hands my
own hands stained with ink": Graphic
Studio, Dublin, and the origins of fine-
art printmaking in Ireland

Conor Lucey
The Stapleton collection of drawings in
the National Library of Ireland

Terry Dolan
Language wars: English versus Irish

Maurice Harmon
Richard Murphy: a poet in good form
With a reading of Murphy's poetry
by Patrick Semple

Marie Coleman
Advertising the Irish Sweepstakes

Declan Downey
Within the strategic elites: Irish nobility
integrated in Brussels, Madrid and
Vienna, c.1600-1800

2008
Tom Dunne
Irish and British history in the paintings
of Daniel Maclise

Richard Aldous
The rivals are immortal: Gladstone
and Disraeli

Ciara Breathnach
"There'll be war there yet": intestacy
in twentieth-century Ireland
Published as "An exploration of
bequeathing patterns in twentieth-
century Ireland" in *The History of the*
Family: an international quarterly,
14:3 (2009)

Maeve O'Sullivan
"News that stays news": the response
of poets to three tragedies

2009
Patrick Geoghegan
"The Mob King": Daniel O'Connell
and the making of Ireland

Mark O'Brien
The history of the "Irish Times"

Michael Kennedy
The Chief of Staff's Reports, 1940-1949

Ronan Fanning
The hunt for Eliza Lynch

Felix M. Larkin
Artistic bombs: the Shemus cartoons
in the "Freeman's Journal", 1920-1924
Mr Larkin's book on the Shemus
cartoons, *Terror and Discord*, was
launched by Nicholas Robinson after
this lecture

Appendix 2

The Richard Irvine Best Memorial Lectures

This lecture series was set up by the National Library of Ireland as a result of a bequest from the American academic, Professor Vernam Hull. The lectures commemorate Richard Irvine Best, who was the fourth Librarian of the Library from 1924 to 1940. The title of his post was changed to Director during his term of office. He also held a chair in the School of Celtic Studies at the Dublin Institute for Advanced Studies, and was Chairman of the Irish Manuscripts Commission. In 2000 additional funding for the continuance of the series was obtained from the National Library Trust Fund. The lectures given to date are listed hereunder.

1969
Daniel A. Binchy
Richard Irvine Best

1971
David Greene
Richard Irvine Best and the
organisation of Irish scholarship

1973
Brian Ó Cuív
The Irish Bardic Duanaire or "Poem
Book"

1975
Palle Birklund
(Danish National Librarian)
The role of the national library today

1977
Terence de Vere White
R.I. Best and his literary contemporaries
Published in *Irish University Review*,
7:2 (Autumn 1997)

1979
Gearóid Mac Niocaill
Religious literature and practice in late
medieval Ireland

1982
W.B. Stanford
Ulysses from Homer to Joyce

1984
Nessa Ní Shéaghdha
Collectors of Gaelic manuscripts,
motives and methods
Published by the Dublin Institute
for Advanced Studies (1985)

1986
Vivian Mercier
Beckett and the Bible

1989
Portia Robinson
Irish and Australians: in the beginning

1993
Seamus Heaney
A torchlight procession of one: Hugh
MacDiarmid

1996
Julia Neuberger
(Chancellor, University of Ulster)
On being Jewish

2000
Michael Holroyd
George Bernard Shaw

2002
Máirtín Ó Murchú
*The Society for the Preservation
of the Irish Language*

2004
Roy Foster
*The gift of adaptability: Yeats, Joyce
and Irish independence*

2006
Vigdis Moe Skarstein
(National Librarian of Norway)
*Knowledge and culture: the National
Library of Norway into the twenty-first
century*
This lecture coincided with the State
Visit to Ireland by Their Majesties
King Harald V and Queen Sonja of
Norway, during which Queen Sonja
visited the National Library of Ireland
to open an exhibition to mark the
centenary of the death of Henrik Ibsen

2009
Robert P. Schmuhl
*Easter 1916 and America: a provisional
appraisal*

Appendix 3

The Professor John J. O'Meara Memorial Lecture series

John J. O'Meara died in 2003. He was Professor of Latin at UCD from 1948 to 1984. His published works include studies of St Augustine and Eriugena and translations of *The Voyage of St Brendan* and the *Topographia Hiberniae* of Giraldus Cambrensis, as well as papers dealing with education in Ireland. He was a close friend of Patrick Henchy, the founder of the National Library of Ireland Society, and supported the Society on its foundation.

Having presented their father's archive to the National Library, his family also endowed a series of lectures to be delivered in his memory. The Director of the National Library entrusted the organisation of these lectures to the National Library of Ireland Society. Details of the five lectures delivered to date are given here. It must be mentioned that the organisation of these lectures was almost entirely the work of Felix M. Larkin, Vice-Chairman of the Society.

2005
Mary Beard
The Roman triumph
(The inaugural lecture)
Published in Felix M. Larkin (ed.),
Librarians, Poets and Scholars:
a Festschrift for Dónall Ó Luanaigh
(Dublin, 2007)

2007
Denis Donoghue
The Latin factor: a chapter of
autobiography
Published as "Chapter 2: The Latin
factor" in Denis Donoghue, *On*
Eloquence (New Haven & London,
2008)

2008
Eamon Duffy
Latin and the Mass: should we mind,
and does it matter?

2009
Mary Carruthers
"To make a library of my memory": the
transmission and invention of knowledge
in the Middle Ages.

2010
Most Rev. Diarmuid Martin,
Archbishop of Dublin
If Newman were around today:
reflections on higher education in the
twenty-first century
Published on the website of the
Archdiocese of Dublin,
www.dublindiocese.ie

Sources

This account of the history of the National Library of Ireland Society is based on the archive of the National Library of Ireland Society which covers the years from its foundation to date. The archive to 1998 has been donated to the National Library of Ireland and is now in the Department of Manuscripts. Applications to consult the archive should be addressed to: The Keeper of Manuscripts, National Library of Ireland, Kildare Street, Dublin 2.

Acknowledgements

Firstly, I wish to acknowledge the assistance of Gerard Lyne, Keeper of Manuscripts in the National Library until May 2009, and his staff – Ciara Kerrigan (who is also a former Honorary Secretary of the Society), Colette O'Daly, Thomas Desmond and all the Library Assistants of the Department.

I am much indebted to other former Honorary Secretaries of the Society – Sandra McDermott, Colette O'Flaherty and Gerard Long – and to the present Secretary, Roger Courtney. My thanks are also due to Honora Faul, Curator of Prints and Drawings in the Library.

I wish to thank the following members of the Executive Committee of the Society, both past and present, who kindly placed their knowledge at my disposal: Fr J. Anthony Gaughan, Professor Maurice Harmon, Mrs Monica Henchy, Dr Margaret Mac Curtain OP and Mrs Veronica McEvatt. I am also grateful to Fr Gaughan for so kindly contributing the Foreword to this book and for assistance with proof-reading.

As always Kevin Browne, the Library's Operations Manager, was most helpful. The present Director of the Library, Fiona Ross, and her predecessor, Aongus Ó hAonghusa, were very supportive of the project. Many thanks also to Brian McKenna, Keeper of Printed Books, and Noel Stapleton, Executive Officer, Microfilm Unit, for their kind assistance on a number of occasions.

I thank the Board of the National Library of Ireland for allowing me to quote from material in the National Library of Ireland archive. Moreover, I am grateful to the Board of the National Library of Ireland and to Imelda Healy, Brian Lalor, Pat Liddy, Alison Countess of Rosse, and Dr Thomas Ryan for permission to reproduce images in this book. My thanks also to Fr Paul Murphy OFM Cap.

I wish to thank Felix M. Larkin whose idea this history was and who monitored my progress very well. He compiled the index. Dr Ian d'Alton also assisted in the final stages before publication.

Lastly, my wife Mary always provided me with encouragement and asked the right questions.

Index

Pages in bold refer to illustrations

Adams, Michael 43
Ainsworth, Anita Lady 40
Ainsworth, Sir John F., Bart 22, 40
Allberry, E. Hilda 6, 26
Andrews, C.S. 14
Archer, William 35
Armstrong, Jonathan 25
Arnold, Bruce 13, 16
Austen, Jane 36

Banotti, Mary, MEP 37
Banville, John 10
Barrington, Tom 14
Bartlett, Thomas 39
Beckett, John 18
Behan, Anthony **33**
Best, Richard Irvine 10, 17, 20, 57
Blaeu, Joan 44
Blair, Ciarán 23, 24
Blunden, Bernadette 38
Blunden, Dermot 11, **29**, 37, 38
Boland, Eavan 10
Bradshaw, Brendan 10
Brontë family 44
Brown, J. Barry 11, 25–26
Brown, Stephen, SJ 21, 25
Brown, Wanda Petronella 6, 11,
    20, 25
Bruton, John, TD 9, 17, 42
Butler, Hubert 25
Butler, Patricia 37

Calvert, Irene 15
Cassells, Peter 37
Charlton, Jack 20
Chubb, Margot 14
Clarke, Desmond 5, 9, 13, 14, 16, 17, 19,
    21, 23, **27**
Comerford, Máire 13
Cook, Pat 36
Costello, Con, Col. **30**
Costello, Peter 5, 9
Courtney, Roger 40
Craig, Maurice J. 9, 16, 18, 22, 25, 36
Cromien, Seán 39
Cruise O'Brien, Máire 13
Cusack, Cyril 18
Cussen, Robert 15

d'Alton, Ian 11, 44
Darwin, Kenneth 14
de Bhaldraithe, Tomás 13
de Courcy, J.W. (Seán) 9, 25, **28**, 36, 38
de Courcy, Sheila **28**
de Valera, Éamon, President of
    Ireland 39
Denvir, Gearóid 10
Diamond, Jason 44
Donlon, Patricia **28**, 35, 37, 39, 45
Duffy, Eamon **34**

Eager, Alan 13
Edgeworth, Maria 39

Edgeworth, Richard Lowell 21
Ellmann, Richard 8, 14
Elmes, Rosalind M. 18

Finegan, Francis, SJ 13
Fitzelle, Brian 23, 24
FitzGerald, Garret, TD 15
Foster, Roy 10

Galvin, Sir John 15
Gannon, Cathal 18
Garvin, Kathleen 23
Garvin, Tom 10, 52
Gaughan, J. Anthony, Fr 5–6, 9,
    24, **34**, 40, 43
Gilmartin, John 23, 24
Goldberg, Gerald 15
Gorham, Maurice 18
Goulding, John T. 39
Greene, David 8, 14, 23
Griffith, Arthur 36

Harmon, Maurice 10, 14
Hayes, Richard J. 8
Hayes-McCoy, G.A. 13
Heaney, Seamus 10, 12, 23, 43
Heffernan, Kevin 20
Henchy, Monica **28**, 40
Henchy, Patrick 5, 7, 8, 11, 12, 13, 14, 15,
    16, 18, 20, 26, **27**, 37, 40, 41, 59
Hewson, Michael 11, 15, 18, 23, 35
Hickey, Kieran 10, 18, **27**, 37
Holroyd, Michael 17
Hughes, Anthony J. 41
Hull, Vernam 57
Humphreys, Kenneth W. 15, 16
Hyland, Jack 11

Johnston, Jennifer 10
Joly, Jasper Robert 18
Jordan, Neil 10
Joyce, James 14, 18, 36

Kearney, Stephen 24
Kelleher, Mary 43
Kelly, Peter, Mr Justice **34**
Kennelly, Brendan 10, 23
Keogh, Daire **30**
Kerrigan, Ciara **32**, **33**, 40
Kiberd, Declan 10
Kidney, Declan 20
Kiely, Benedict 10, 23
Kissane, Noel 17, 21, 43

Laffan, Michael 10
Lalor, Brian **31**, 39
Lalor, James Fintan 39
Lambert, Eric, TD 9, 21
Larkin, Felix M. 6, 11, 12, **33**, 41, 43,
    44, 59
Lavin, Mary 18
Le Brocquy, Sybil 18
Ledwidge, Francis 44
Lee, J.J. 10
Lefroy, Thomas, Lord Chief Justice 36
L'Estrange, Gerard, TD 13
Lewis, C.S. 43
Line, Maurice B. 35
Long, Gerard **32**, **33**, 39
Longford, Earl of: see Pakenham, Frank
Longley, Michael 10
Lynch, Brian 37
Lynch, Patrick 8, 13, 14, 16, 19, **27**
Lyne, Gerard 6, 11, 23, **30**, **34**, 36, 39
Lysaght, Charles E. 26

Mac An Ailí, Ciarán 8, 14

McCarthy, Muriel 5, 9, **33**, 44

McCarthy, Niall, Mr Justice 25

McCarville, Eileen 15

Mac Conghail, Máire **33**

Mac Conghail, Muiris 10

Mac Curtain, Margaret, OP 9, 15, **30**, 38, 40, 41

McDermott, Sandra **32**, **33**, 40, 41

McEvatt, Veronica 15, 24, 40

McGartoll, Statia 24

McGlinchey, Tadhg 14, 20, 27

McGuire, James 43

McKiernan, Eoin 8, 14, 15

Mac Lochlainn, Alf 8, 12, 20, 21, 23, **28**, 38

MacLysaght, Edward 15, 26

Malone, J.B. 21

Manning, Maurice, Senator 37

Murphy, Brian 41

Nealon, Ted, TD 26

Nevin, Monica 24

Ní Shéaghdha, Nessa 10

Ní Shúilliobhán, Nora 6, 11, 16–17, **30**, 37, 40

O'Brien, Edna 18

Ó Braonáin, Annraí 6, 44

O'Byrne, Máirín 14

O'Conor Don family 37

Ó Cuív, Brian 17, 20

Ó Dálaigh, Cearbhall, Chief Justice and President of Ireland 8, 14

O'Daly, Colette **32**, **33**

O'Donnell, Peader 12

O Donoghue, Brendan 39, 41

O'Driscoll, Robert 13

Ó Dúill, Gréagóir 24

O'Faolain, Sean 18

O'Ferrall, Edward More 24

O'Flaherty, Colette 39

Ó hAonghusa, Aongus **34**, 41

Ó hEocha, Colm 14

Ó hÓgartaigh, Ciarán 11, 38, 41

Ó hUaithne, Dáithí: see Greene, David

O'Leary, Liam 36

Ó Luanaigh, Dónall 5–6, 12, 23, **29**, **33**, 36, 38, 43

Ó Luanaigh, Mary **33**

Ó Lúing, Seán 26, **28**, **29**, 37, 39

O'Mahony, Eoin 16

O'Mahony, Peter Tynan 26, 38

Ó Maitiú, Séamus **32**

O'Meara, John J. 6, 10, 14–15, 42, 59

O'Meara, Odile 6, **34**

Ó Mórdha, Seán 10

O'Neill, Thomas P. 38–9

O'Sullivan, Harold 38

Pakenham, Frank, Earl of Longford 39

Pakenham, Thomas **32**, 44

Parke, H.W. 14

Pearse, Patrick 36

Pollard, Mary P. (Paul) 43

Power, Ellen 14

Prior, Thomas 21

Purser, Sarah 7

Pyle, Hilary 13

Reynolds, Lorna 12

Robinson, Mary, President of Ireland **28**, 37, 44

Robinson, Nicholas 44

Rose, David 24
Ryan, Eoin, Senator 13
Ryan, Thomas, PPRHA 26

Sadleir, Randal 42
Sadleir, Thomas Ulick 42
Scannell, Mary J.P. 41
Schmuhl, Robert P. 17
Shaw, George Bernard 17
Sheehy Skeffington, Andrée **28**, 38
Sheehy Skeffington, Francis 36
Sheehy Skeffington, Hanna 36
Sheehy Skeffington, Owen, Senator 13
Smith, Cornelius F. 25
Smith, Jean Kennedy 38
Swords, Liam, Fr 10

Turpin, John 41

Uí Bhraonáin, Donla 6, 44

Walton, Julian 24
Wheeler, Gordon 44
Wheeler, Henry A. 9, 22, 23, 25, 36
Wilde, Oscar 24
Williams, T. Desmond 15
Wilson, John, TD 22
Woolf, E. Maitland 24

Yeats, Anne 40
Yeats, Gráinne 40
Yeats, Michael 8, 13, 14, **27**, 40
Yeats, William Butler 14, 40